10/05

Floods

Floods

Lisa Trumbauer

Franklin Watts
A Division of Scholastic Inc.
New York • Toronto • London • Auckland • Sydney
Mexico City • New Delhi • Hong Kong
Danbury, Connecticut

For my in-laws, David and Randi Trumbauer

Note to readers: Definitions for words in **bold** can be found in the Glossary at the back of this book.

Photographs © 2005: AP/Wide World Photos: 28 (Steve Helber), cover (Charlie Riedel), 50 (Wally Santana), 2 (Karen Tam), 20 (Ted S. Warren); Bruce Coleman Inc.: 12 (Byron Jorjorian), 42 (Drew Thate); Corbis Images: 48 (Kevin Fleming), 33 (T. Gerson/L.A. Daily News/Sygma), 36 (John Heseltine), 5 right, 26 (NOAA/Reuters), 49 (Tim Page), 10 (Tom Pietrasik), 22, 30, 40, 45 (Reuters), 17 (Joel W. Rogers), 34, 35 (Royalty-Free), 51 (Michael T. Sedam), 16 (Richard Hamilton Smith), 23 (Les Stone), 24 (Vince Streano), 5 left, 44 (A & J Verkaik), 41; Getty Images/Graeme Robertson: 21; ImageState/Jim Russi: 9; The Image Works: 47 (Brigitte Deconinck), 38 (Judy Glasel), 14 (Andrew Holbrook), 46 (Frank Pedrick), 31 (Sean Ramsay), 27 (Tony Savino); TRIP Photo Library: 8 (D. Burrows), 18 (Bob Turner), 6; U.S. Bureau of Reclamation: 39; Visuals Unlimited/Melvin Zucker: 32.

Illustration by Bob Italiano

The photograph on the cover shows a boater traveling to a home in Albany, Illinois, flooded by the Mississippi River in 2001. The photograph opposite the title page shows a row of homes in Tarboro, North Carolina, surrounded by the floodwaters left by Hurricane Floyd in 1999.

Library of Congress Cataloging-in-Publication Data

Trumbauer, Lisa, 1963–
  Floods / Lisa Trumbauer.
    p. cm. — (Watts library)
  Includes bibliographical references and index.
  ISBN 0-531-12283-2
  1. Floods—Juvenile literature. I. Title. II. Series.
  GB1399.T78 2005
  551.48'9—dc22   2005000913

1 2 3 4 5 6 7 8 9 10 R 14 13 12 11 10 09 08 07 06 05

Contents

Chapter One
Water, Water Everywhere   7

Chapter Two
River Flooding 15

Chapter Three
Weathering the Big Storms 25

Chapter Four
Taming the Wild Rivers 35

Chapter Five
Flood Forecasts 43

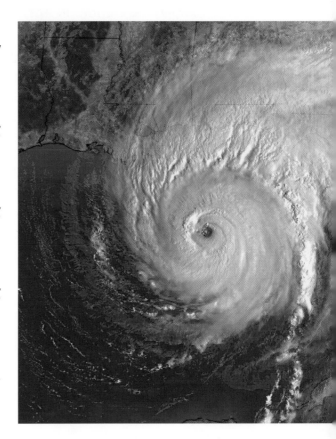

52 **Timeline**

53 **Glossary**

57 **To Find Out More**

60 **A Note on Sources**

61 **Index**

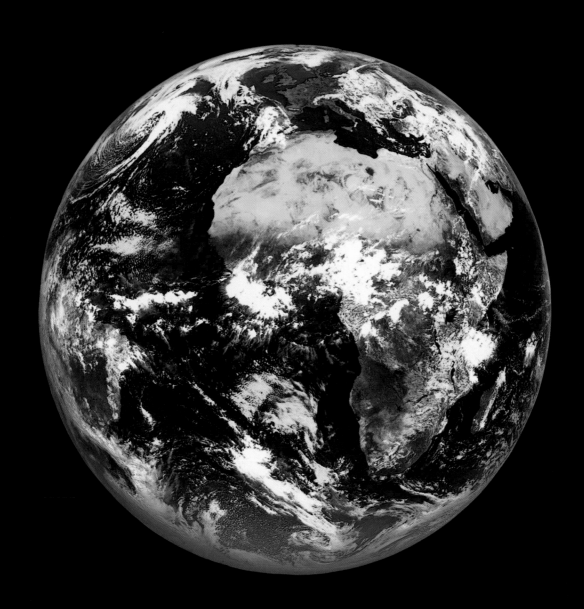

As this view of Earth from space shows, water covers much of the planet.

Chapter One

Water, Water Everywhere

With so much land around us, it is sometimes hard to remember that our world is mostly covered by water. If you look at a world map, you can see how much water surrounds the continents and how much water weaves in and out of the land.

Sometimes the water on our planet runs wild. Waves far out in the ocean can roll forward until they engulf entire beaches. Rivers swell up and overflow their banks, flooding farms and communities. Fierce storms unleash torrential downpours and whip up ocean waves. And each time the water runs wild, we must try to understand how it happened and how we can protect ourselves better the next time.

What causes **floods**? Too much rain or rain combined with melting snow causes some floods. **Hurricanes** and **tsunamis** also cause floods. Still other floods are caused when a **dam** or other structure fails to control the flow of river water. No matter what causes a flood, we all must learn to live with the consequences.

Flooding has turned this main street into a deserted canal.

An ocean wave can be beautiful—and dangerously powerful, especially during a storm.

Awesome Oceans

Exactly how much of our planet do you think is covered by water? Water covers nearly 71 percent of Earth's surface. Of that percentage, 97 percent of all the water found on Earth is ocean water. In fact, you could almost look at the continents as islands on Earth, surrounded by water.

If you were sitting on a beach, watching the ocean, what is the first thing you might notice? Probably the waves, right?

Waves occur because of two forces—wind and gravity. When the wind blows, it pushes the water upward, creating the high part of a wave, called the **crest.** Gravity then pulls the wave back down. Boats on the open ocean feel the waves as an up-and-down motion. During a storm, a wave may be as tall as 40 feet (12 meters)—about as tall as a four-story building. Sailors at sea are very aware of the ocean's powers and the dangers of those powers.

After the 2004 Indian Ocean tsunami, barely any houses were left on this street in Hambantota, Sri Lanka. The tsunami struck on a busy market day and drowned many of the victims.

Deadly Tsunamis

The most dangerous waves on the planet are tsunamis. They are formed by tremors or **earthquakes** that occur deep in the ocean, hundreds of feet below the surface. At first, the waves might be barely noticeable. But the tsunami wave travels about 600 miles (965 kilometers) an hour. As the water becomes less deep, the wave's height builds. By the time it reaches land, the wave may be as high as 50 feet (15 m) or more.

Tsunamis can cause horrific damage once they reach shore. The Indian Ocean earthquake and resulting tsunami of December 26, 2004, proved that. Somewhere between 200,000 and 300,000 people are thought to have died in this tragedy.

Indian Ocean Tsunami

The morning of December 26, 2004, was quiet and beautiful. The sun shone brightly over the beaches of South Asia, a popular destination for tourists. Many people—vacationers and locals alike—were enjoying their breakfasts. Some families were already out early, their children playing on the beaches. It was an idyllic tropical morning.

Suddenly, the ocean pulled back from the beach, as if something had sucked it out to sea. Fish flapped on the sand, and people rushed up to see this remarkable sight. Then the ground began to tremble, and out on the ocean, a large wall of water could be seen, making its deadly way toward shore.

Families scrambled away from the beach, dragging children and clutching their belongings. People on hotel balconies watched as a giant wall of water rose and fell across the beach, then rushed up to flood hotel patios and pools. People clung to palm trees, railings, and anything else they could grab hold of as the force of the water pummeled and pulled at them. No one quite understood what was happening. It wasn't a storm, because the sky was clear. So why did the ocean suddenly fling itself across South Asia that morning?

This was no ordinary wave. It was a tsunami, and it had been triggered by an earthquake along the floor of the Indian Ocean. The wave devastated many areas of South Asia, including Thailand, Malaysia, Sri Lanka, Indonesia, and India. About 70 percent of the residents of Sumatra, an island in Indonesia, died. The city of Banda Aceh was destroyed. Buildings were demolished and washed away. Many people were never seen again. The tsunami wave completely flooded the town, with water cresting as high as palm trees. The Indian Ocean tsunami is one of the largest natural disasters of modern history—the final death toll could total more than a quarter of a million people.

Water cascades down from the mountains at Yosemite National Park in California.

Earth's Other Water Sources

If 97 percent of all the water found on Earth comes from the oceans, where does the remaining 3 percent come from? Part of it is from lakes and rivers.

Most natural lakes were formed long ago, when Earth was covered by glaciers. As the glaciers melted, they left behind large bodies of water and exposed land, which surrounded the water. These water bodies became lakes.

Rivers also form on land. Most rivers begin as small **rivulets,** often high in the mountains. As gravity pulls the water down the mountain, the rivulet joins with other rivulets to form a bigger brook. As they continue their journey downward, brooks and streams ultimately meet to form a river.

Rivers affect the land, carving away the soil, winding around hills, and flowing over steep cliffs as waterfalls. Rivers also react to changes in their environment. Too much rain may cause a river to flood. A human-made dam may cause a river to change its course. Too little rain may cause the level of the river to drop. Weather is an important component of understanding a river's capacity to overflow.

The Water Cycle

Have you ever noticed that after a rainstorm, the rain-drenched streets soon become dry? Why does this happen? It's all part of the **water cycle.**

The water cycle is the process that shapes our weather. As heat from the sun warms up the water on Earth, the water changes to a gas called **water vapor.** Outdoors, the water vapor rises into the air, where it begins to cool.

As the water vapor cools, it changes, or **condenses,** into

water droplets. These water droplets form clouds. Then the clouds deposit moisture back to Earth as **precipitation** in the form of rain or snow. It falls in the ocean or on land, eventually ending up in the ocean, completing the cycle.

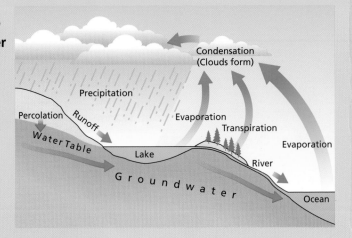

Condensation (Clouds form)

Precipitation

Percolation

Runoff

Water Table

Evaporation

Transpiration

Evaporation

Lake

River

G r o u n d w a t e r

Ocean

Life's Necessity

Water is necessary for life. Plants need water to grow. People and animals need water to drink. Without water, our world would be as lifeless as the other planets in our solar system. In fact, what those planets mostly lack is water. Yet for all its life-giving abilities, water can be a dangerous foe, especially when the waters on Earth run wild and flood. Let's learn more about how the waters rage out of control.

Water in Air

Do you know that the air we breathe contains water? Air is made up of mostly gases—78 percent nitrogen and 21 percent oxygen. The remaining 1 percent contains a few other gases, including water vapor. That's the gas form of water!

Floodwaters cover these fields in the midwestern United States.

Chapter Two

River Flooding

"Rain, rain, go away. Come again some other day." Do you remember chanting these words when you were young? For people whose lands are on the verge of flooding, these words are more than a childhood nursery rhyme. They are a demand for the rain to cease so their homes, fields, and streets won't be flooded.

Rain is necessary for life on Earth. Farmers especially need rain to grow crops. But what happens if it keeps

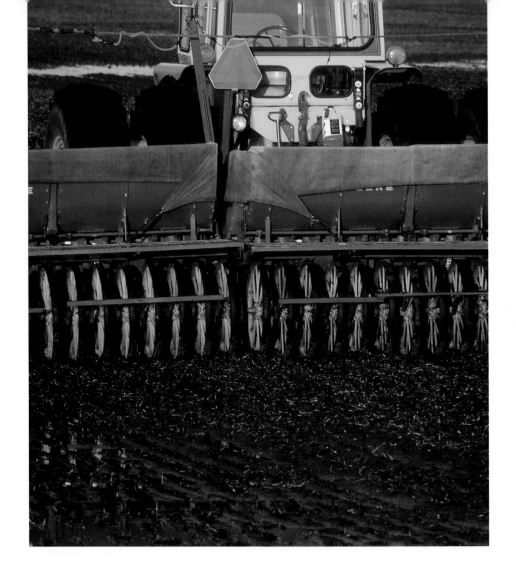

After the land has absorbed as much rain as it can, puddles begin to form on the ground. If it continues to rain, flooding can result.

raining? The land can hold only so much water. When the land has reached its limit, the rainwater begins to flow over the land, or flood.

You might have witnessed this yourself on a much smaller scale. Have you ever noticed that when it rains, puddles sometimes form at the bottom of grassy hills or in low areas of a lawn or field? The ground was not able to absorb all the rainwater, and it created a puddle, or a miniature flood.

On a bigger scale, flooding from too much rain may create rivulets of water across the land. These rivulets are called **runoff.** Runoff water may wash away plants and cause serious damage to farms. As runoff joins with smaller brooks and then larger streams, the brooks and streams become bigger. The streams eventually lead to a river, above-ground or underground. The heavy rainfall combined with the increased amount of water in a river's **tributaries** can cause a river to overflow its banks and flood the land.

Floods that occur due to too much rain or **snowmelt** are sometimes called **river floods.** When the snow melts too quickly or the rain falls too heavily, the land cannot absorb all the water and the rivers cannot contain all the water. In addition, the ground may still be frozen, further preventing absorption. Flooding is the end result.

This aerial view shows how brooks join up to form a river. Extra rainwater in a river's tributaries can contribute to river flooding.

Good Floods

Floods aren't always destructive. Take the longest river in the world—the Nile River, which flows 4,160 miles (6,693 km) through Egypt and Sudan. Throughout history, the Nile flooded every spring. The flooding ultimately benefited the land by redistributing fertile soil to the Egyptian plains. The Aswan High Dam, opened in 1968, now mostly controls the flooding.

What Is the Floodplain?

Low lands that lie along rivers are naturally prone to flooding, especially in the spring when winter snows melt and spring rains fall. These lands are called the **floodplains.**

Many homes and farms are built along floodplains. But if you know the land is going to flood, why would you live on a floodplain? A modest amount of flooding is actually good for the soil. The river waters bring nutrients and rich soil to the land, which helps crops and other plants grow. The rich soil and an abundant water supply make living along the floodplains often worth the risks.

To protect themselves from harmful floodwaters, people often build **levees** along the river. A levee is a riverbank built up by people to confine the river water. Most of the time, the levee will hold and the river water will remain within the boundaries of the river. However, when the river water rises above the levee, the water overflows and causes flooding.

Water Jams

Sometimes floods occur because ice or **debris** has jammed the flow of a river. During the winter, brooks and streams in the north or at higher mountain altitudes can freeze. As the streams begin to thaw, big ice chunks can dislodge and flow downstream. These chunks of ice can jam up in shallow water, along narrow parts in the river, or perhaps even along bridge piers.

When this happens, water builds up behind the ice. When the force of the water becomes too strong, the ice is too weak to hold it. As the ice breaks, the water rushes through in quantities that are much larger than the normal flow of the river.

This sudden burst of water causes flooding. The solid blocks of ice rushing along with the water are an additional danger.

Debris floods are similar in nature to ice-jam floods. Instead of ice, debris jams the flow of a river. Land debris includes trees, rocks, sand, or mud. Water builds behind the jam and eventually breaks through and floods the area.

A worker stands in a boat to clear an enormous jam of logs near Everett, Washington. The debris washed down the Snohomish River during several days of heavy rain and flooding.

Flash floods can be extremely destructive. After two hours of heavy rain, flooding swept away buildings and cars in the English village of North Cornwell in 2004.

Flash Flood!

Water jams can cause the most dangerous flood of all—a **flash flood.** Heavy rains that fall in a very short period of time can also cause flash flooding. A flash flood is not a slow, steady flooding of the land or rising of a river, but a sudden release of water. A flash flood can be powerful enough to knock over trees, topple buildings, rip bridges from their moorings, and wash away cars, buses, and trucks in its path.

A homeowner cleans up after a flash flood sent a wall of water 12 feet (4 m) high through Mullens, West Virginia. The 2001 flood destroyed the town's business district and left many residents homeless.

Flash floods are extremely dangerous and often hard to predict. The gush of river water from a flash flood can hit unexpectedly, flooding towns and homes and causing damage to property and injury to people.

In 1972, a flash flood in Rapid City, South Dakota, killed 238 people. The flash flood occurred when 15 inches (38 centimeters) of rain fell in about six hours, forcing Rapid Creek to overflow its banks. It ranks as one of the country's most deadly and expensive floods.

Cities are often more prone to flooding because they don't have soil-covered ground to absorb the water from a flash flood. Cement streets and city sidewalks are not absorbent. Instead, cities have sewers for floodwaters to run into. But if too much water rushes through the streets too quickly, the sewers may not be able to hold all the water, and the powerful runoff floods the streets.

The Great Flood of 1993

The states in the Midwest along the Mississippi River and its tributaries experienced an unusually wet summer in 1993. The rain began to fall and, in one instance, didn't stop for twenty days. The amount of rain that fell was at least 200 percent more than normal that summer. Consequently, the land could not hold much water, and the rivers began to overflow. The levees—which people worked tirelessly to strengthen and heighten—were no match for the swollen rivers. The river water continued to rise and eventually broke through the levees, and flash flooding occurred. The floods were unstoppable.

By the end of the summer, fifty people had lost their lives, about ten thousand homes were completely destroyed, and some 15 million acres (6 million hectares) of farmland were underwater. The Great Flood of 1993—a river flood combined with flash floods—was one of the most destructive floods ever to hit the United States.

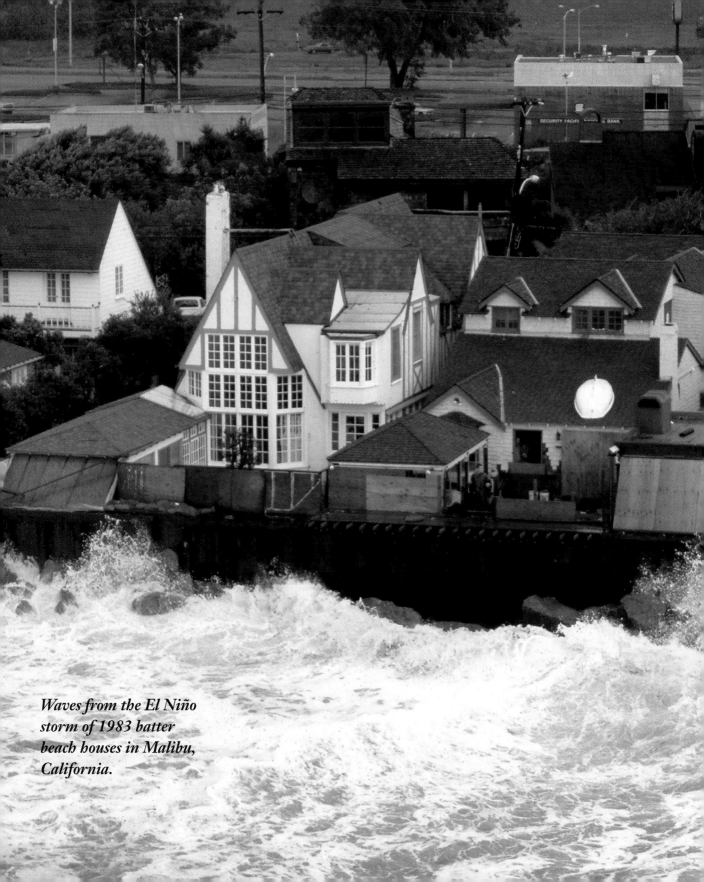

Waves from the El Niño storm of 1983 batter beach houses in Malibu, California.

Chapter Three

Weathering the Big Storms

Land along rivers is not the only place that faces the threat of floods. Communities along the seacoast are also threatened by floods. Here, instead of too much rain or snowmelt, a force of nature that brings strong wind, pounding rains, thunder, and lightning causes floods. This impressive force of nature is, of course, a hurricane.

Out at Sea

One reason why hurricanes pack such a wallop is because they develop over the open ocean—where most of the water on the planet is contained. Hurricanes begin as storms called **tropical storms.** Warm air over the ocean surface causes the water to evaporate quickly, and the warmth and moisture in the air rise in a spiral to form a storm. Tropical storms and hurricanes often occur in late summer and early fall because water temperatures must be warm for these storms to develop.

During a tropical storm, winds travel around in a whirlpool-like motion, called a **vortex.** This vortex includes a

A satellite image of Hurricane Ivan on September 15, 2004, shows the vortex of the dangerous storm as it moved toward the Gulf Coast.

center, or an **eye,** which often does not have clouds. Tropical storms have wind speeds of more than 39 miles (63 km) per hour but don't yet have the intensity of a hurricane. A tropical storm may be as wide as 200 miles (322 km).

A storm officially becomes a hurricane when its winds reach a speed of 74 miles (119 km) per hour. Such powerful winds can blow over trees and road signs and affect the ocean, creating incredibly tall waves that crash on the shore. The huge amount of rain produced by the storm can also force streams and lakes to overflow and flood the land.

Floods caused by ocean waves from hurricanes or tropical storms are called **storm-surge floods.** An abnormal rise in sea level during a hurricane or tropical storm is to blame. The worst single natural disaster in U.S. history was the result of a storm surge. On September 8, 1900, more than six thousand people died when a hurricane and its storm surge hit Galveston, Texas. That's more than four times the number of people who died when the *Titanic* sank.

Hurricanes can cause storm-surge floods. This house was flooded by Hurricane Opal in Florida in 1995.

Flooding caused by Hurricane Floyd covers Franklin, Virginia. Floyd passed through the area in a single day, but it generated rain for several days before its arrival.

Different Names

Hurricanes develop in the North Atlantic and eastern Pacific oceans. Typhoons and tropical cyclones are hurricanes that develop in different parts of the world. Typhoons are born in the western North Pacific Ocean and the south China Sea. Tropical cyclones originate in the Indian Ocean and off the northwest Australian coast.

Hurricane Floyd

In September 1999, North Carolina was hit by not one but two fierce storms. On September 5, Hurricane Dennis arrived and was quickly **downgraded** to Tropical Storm Dennis. The land and the rivers were able to absorb the 6 inches (15 cm) of Dennis's rainwater. However, ten days later, a second hurricane—Hurricane Floyd—developed.

Hurricane Floyd struck the North Carolina coast in the early morning hours of September 16, 1999. Over the next twelve hours, it let loose between 15 and 20 inches (38 and 51 cm) of rain. It didn't take long for Hurricane Floyd to move through the state, and by midday on September 16, the sun began to shine.

But the severe aftereffects of Hurricane Floyd had not yet been felt. Later that night, four rivers in North Carolina—the Tar, the Neuse, the Roanoke, and the Pamlico—and their tributaries overflowed. The floodwaters rose so high and so quickly that people didn't have time to escape. Many residents had no option but to sit on the roofs of their homes. Roads were quickly flooded, preventing people from fleeing by car. The rushing waters coursed through sewage plants and local farms, contaminating the water supply. Floodwaters rose, or crested, as high as 24 feet (7 m) in some areas and nearly wiped

Statistically Speaking

Scientists say that Hurricane Floyd created a so-called 500-year flood. Although you might think that means a similar flood wouldn't occur for another 500 years, it actually describes the probability of a flood of that magnitude happening in any given year. That is, during any year, there is a 1-in-500, or 0.2 percent, chance that a flood like the one in North Carolina after Hurricane Floyd would happen again.

Sometimes floods are called 100-year floods. This means that during any given year, there is a 1-in-100, or a 1 percent, chance that a flood will occur. So, even though a major flood may have just occurred, a flood of the same strength could come again within 100—or even 500—years. But the chances are very slim!

After Hurricane Floyd struck, hogs from a farm near Trenton, North Carolina, wait for rescue on top of their barn. Floodwaters claim hogs too tired to swim anymore.

out the town of Princeville.

Fifty-two people died because of Hurricane Floyd, many of whom were victims of the unexpected and fast-rising floodwaters. One disturbing image of the hurricane showed flooded farms on which hundreds of thousands of pigs had drowned. Experts estimate that the hurricane and its aftermath cost the state about $4.5 billion.

Flooding caused by El Niño storms in Lakeport, California, allows local children to paddle a boat in a park now underwater.

Losing Power

Hurricanes thrive on the water they receive from the ocean. Once the storm reaches land, that water is no longer available, and the hurricane begins to lose its punch.

El Niño—A Troublesome "Child"

It's clear that ocean waters play an important role in forming hurricanes and tropical storms. **El Niño** (pronounced EL NEEN-yoe) is a phenomenon that occurs in the Pacific Ocean when water along the equator becomes warmer than normal. Fishers in Ecuador and Peru named these warm ocean waters El Niño, which is Spanish for "boy child" or "Christ child," because the warm waters first arrived at Christmastime. These waters can create all sorts of weather havoc, including floods.

Why should warmer ocean water cause weather problems? Remember—as water warms, it evaporates into the air. This warmer water forms clouds, which bring rain. So, warmer water means more clouds, which means more rain. And this rain often falls over areas that normally do not receive a lot of rain, which can cause flooding.

California is one of the states most affected by El Niño. Heavy rains and abnormally large waves create flooding and mud slides there. During the 1998 El Niño season in California, waves crested at 30 feet (9 m). Some 22 inches (56 cm) of rain fell during the first week of February in San Marcos Pass, and 12 inches (30 cm) fell in Ventura. Floodwaters washed away sections of the state's major highways. In the nearby mountains, 3 feet (1 m) of snow fell.

The 1998 El Niño season devastated some parts of California. On February 1, 1998, the huge waves of El Niño destroyed several houses in Malibu.

Because most storms bring some sort of precipitation with them, even blizzards can contribute mightily to the possibility of flooding. But floods can be created by something other than nature—floods can also be created by people.

This dam controls water flow on the Mississippi River in Davenport, Iowa.

Chapter Four

Taming the Wild Rivers

The flow of a river is a powerful force. The river is always moving toward its end, usually the ocean. People often try to control a river's flow by constructing dams or building up levees. Most of the time, a dam or levee can control the river water. But every once in a while, the river's flow is too much for even a dam to hold back. The result is flooding.

Towns and villages are located by rivers for many reasons, including productive farmland, easy access to the water, and the beautiful landscape.

River Life

Living along a river has its rewards and its risks. Lands that border a river often have rich soil, making the earth perfect for planting and growing food. The river itself can be used for drinking water and sometimes as a source of power. Before trains and cars were invented, boats carried people and transported cargo from town to town along the waterways.

It sounds like an idyllic place to live—until the river overflows and floods the land. With so many people depending on the river, it is only natural that people would try to control it. This is achieved by building levees and dams.

Levees and Dams

Levees are the oldest form of flood control. Throughout history, the Dutch have used a kind of levee called a dike to protect their lowlands from the sea. Levees can be made of earth, sand, or concrete. They are human-made structures that prevent flooding when they work and cause flooding when they fail.

Dams are another form of flood control. People build two types of dams: **diversion dams** or **storage dams.** Diversion dams redirect the flow of the river water, usually by controlling how much will flow through the dam at specified times. Storage dams hold back water so that it can be saved for future use.

Flood Proofing

The Federal Emergency Management Agency (FEMA) offers this flood-proofing advice to homeowners on the floodplains:

- Cover the lower exterior of the house with a waterproof coating or cover the lower portion of the building with bricks and seal the spaces between the bricks. To prevent water from seeping in, also fill in any cracks between doors and windows.
- Have a professional contractor put electrical boxes on the second or third floor instead of in a basement or low-level garage. Try to position electric outlets or sockets high up on a wall so floodwater does not soak the outlet holes.
- Floodwaters can damage hot-water heaters as well as heating and cooling units. The safest place for these appliances is on the upper floors rather than in the basement. If appliances cannot be moved, a concrete or brick wall around the appliances to a height consistent with the area's history of flood levels can prevent flood damage.

A reservoir is an artificial lake that serves as a water supply. This reservoir in the town of Olive is part of the New York City water supply system.

Both types of dams can prevent future flooding. For example, in some places, in the spring when rains are more likely and winter snows begin to melt, the river swells with excess water. Storage dams, as well as diversion dams, can store this excess water in **reservoirs** until the water is needed, perhaps during the drier late-summer weeks.

Some diversion dams can also create electricity from the force of the river's flow. Electricity created with the power of water is called **hydroelectricity.** Power that is made by hydroelectricity is called **hydropower.** A power plant needs some type of fuel to turn the turbines in order to generate electricity. That fuel may be burning coal or gas. In the case of a hydropower plant, that fuel may be the force of water. Dams can control the flow of the water, making the water more manageable for the power plant.

But can a river actually be managed and contained by a wall made by people? Sometimes it cannot. And when a dam fails, a flood occurs.

Test the Waters

You see water's power in action every time you wash dishes, the car, even your dog! A trickle of water may not push aside leftover food, dirt, or soap suds. But if you turn up the water and increase the flow, you can see a marked difference in the water's strength. Dam operators try to control the water's strength and flow in a similar way by allowing varying amounts of water to flow through.

This photograph of the view upstream of the Teton Dam failure was taken shortly after the dam collapse on June 5, 1976.

When a Dam Breaks

In 1972, construction began on the Teton Dam. Located on the Teton River in southeast Idaho, the dam was built to fulfill several purposes. Not only would it provide hydropower and water for irrigation, but it would also serve as flood protection. Construction of the dam took four years, and on March 1, 1976, the reservoir created by the dam began filling with water.

Two months later, on June 5, several leaks in the dam were discovered. No one thought the dam was in jeopardy. However by noon, the dam had ruptured and water had broken through. Within five hours, nearly all the water had rushed over the dam, flooding

everything in its path. Although flood warnings had been issued, eleven people perished. Still, experts believe that many more could have died if they had not been warned in time.

From Protection to Devastation

It is difficult to control nature. Even so, dams and levees have been built to do just that. Although dams may be built for different reasons, most are built to prevent flooding. They are designed to withstand a certain amount of pressure from the flowing river water. But when that pressure is greater than the dam's design, the dam will burst. The water that is released is often so powerful that it is capable of causing extreme damage.

So if people can't always control the river or possible floodwaters, how can they protect themselves? Experts have been trying to solve this problem for a long time.

The Johnstown Flood of 1889

The worst flood resulting from a dam failure in the United States occurred in Johnstown, Pennsylvania, on May 31, 1889. The tragedy actually began more than thirty-five years earlier, in 1853, when a dam was built on the South Fork section of the Little Conemaugh River. The dam created a lake, which people used for recreation and fishing. Natural outlets for the lake were screened over so the fish could not escape.

Over the years, lake mud and plants collected against the screens. On May 30, 1889, heavy rains fell, filling up the lake. However, the rainwater had nowhere to go because of the clogged screens. Instead, the water broke through the South Fork Dam, which had not been maintained.

The next day, water rushed southward at a rate of several feet per second, with water as high as 20 to 30 feet (6 to 9 m). Johnstown was about 15 miles (24 km) south of the dam. The flash flood created by the breaking dam swept through the town, killing more than 2,200 people. It was one of the deadliest floods in U.S. history.

Forecasters understand that monitoring river conditions helps prevent damage and injury from flooding.

Chapter Five

Flood Forecasts

As you gaze out at a calm ocean or a gently flowing river, it's hard to imagine that the water can turn wild and dangerous. It's hard to imagine that the height of the water could grow, that the force of the water could become more powerful, that the land nearby could flood in a matter of moments.

We know when a storm comes. We see the dark clouds that will bring rain. We may feel the wind that is the prelude to a tornado. Weather forecasters can see

Dark rain clouds signal bad weather ahead.

the shape of a hurricane from overhead satellites, and they can even fairly predict when a blizzard might arrive. But how can anyone predict when water might run wild and cause a flood?

Learning the River

The National Weather Service runs thirteen River Forecast Centers throughout the United States. In an effort to prevent loss of life and limit property damage during a flood, these centers provide river and flood forecasts and warnings. **Hydrometeorologists** with the centers try to predict flooding by studying not only the nature of a river, but the weather patterns that affect it.

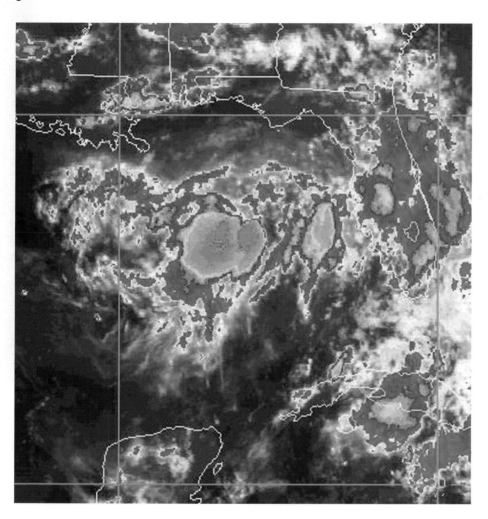

Forecasters at the National Weather Service use satellite images of hurricanes and tropical storms to help predict flooding.

Hydrometeorologists measure the height of river water by placing a gauge along the riverbank and observing how the river rises and falls. The **river stage** is the height of the river measured against a fixed point. In this way, they are able to monitor any changes.

Hydrometeorologists look at a number of factors to determine if a river might flood. One factor is runoff. How much water is moving in from the land due to rain and melting snow? How steeply is the land sloped? What kind of soil is

The rate of rushing water helps hydro-meteorologists forecast river flooding.

Some of the water that fills Ourika Valley in Morocco comes from melted snow. Snowmelt and rainfall amounts, air temperature, soil type, and slope of the land are some factors that determine flood risk.

there? Are there any towns in the runoff's path? When did it last rain, how much rain fell, and how quickly was that rain absorbed into the ground? Also, how warm is the air? How long does the sun shine? That information can help determine how quickly snow might melt.

Another factor is the amount of water coming from upstream. Hydrometeorologists measure the flow of water at a certain point, knowing it must pass farther downstream. They also look at how much water from underground is coming to the surface.

Scientists use this hydraulic model of the Kissimmee River in Florida to better predict the river's behavior under drought and flood conditions.

Hydrometeorologists use models to duplicate the life of a river. These models, combined with extensive tracking of river changes, help hydrometeorologists predict when a river might flood. Experts believe that each year, these predictions help save lives, homes, farmland, and businesses.

What Should You Do?

According to the Federal Emergency Management Agency (FEMA), floods are the most common natural disaster in the

United States. Although any area can be susceptible to flooding, FEMA has mapped out places that have higher chances of flooding. Areas at risk are floodplains and the flatland bordering a river.

Sometimes people underestimate the power of floodwaters. Did you know that 6 inches (15 cm) of swiftly flowing water can knock you down? Or that 2 feet (0.6 m) of water can float a large vehicle such as a bus?

Should you ever find yourself in a flood situation, there are many general safety tips to know. Stay away from the water and get to higher ground. Don't try to outrun a flood or walk through floodwaters. They can be powerful enough to sweep away large structures. Floodwaters could also contain dangerous substances.

Driving through flooded areas is unsafe.

Waves from Typhoon Aere crash against a lighthouse in Taiwan in 2004. In this part of the world, a hurricane is called a typhoon.

Don't ever touch power lines on the ground. People are also encouraged to keep a battery-operated radio nearby to hear updated weather and flood reports, watches, and warnings.

The Worst Flood in History

The worst flood ever recorded occurred in China. During September and October 1887, the Huang He River overflowed. Even though 70-foot (21-m) barriers had been built to hold back the water, the river surged over it. The water flooded about 50,000 square miles (129,500 sq km). No one is sure exactly how many people died, but estimates range from 900,000 to 6 million.

Terms to Know

The term *flood watch* means over-flow of river water is possible within a certain amount of time. The term *flood warning* means flooding is actually taking place or is highly likely in your area.

A *flash-flood watch* means flash flooding is possible in or near your area. *A flash-flood warning* means flash flooding is actually taking place or is highly likely in your area.

Life by the water appeals to many people, including the residents of Provincetown on Cape Cod, Massachusetts.

Beware of Water!

Even though people can't live as fish do, many people are intrigued by the water. They like to live near oceans and build their homes on the shore. They like to live near rivers, where they can fish, farm, or simply enjoy the river's gentle current. They have fun swimming in lakes, surfing the ocean waves, and rafting on rivers.

When the water runs wild, however, nature's strength and power are revealed. River waters and ocean waves may be tamed for a time with dams and seawalls, but they can just as easily rise and flood. Acknowledging the power of water and accepting the possibility of flooding are the first steps to understanding how water can run wild.

Timeline

1887	The Huang He, also known as Yellow River, in China overflows. The death toll is estimated to be between 900,000 and 6 million.
1889	South Fork Dam bursts, creating a flash flood. More than 2,200 people die in Johnstown, Pennsylvania.
1900	More than six thousand are killed in a storm surge that floods Galveston, Texas.
1972	A flash flood in Rapid City, South Dakota, kills 238 people.
1976	Teton Dam in Idaho bursts. The resulting flash flood kills eleven.
1993	The Mississippi River and its tributaries flood, and fifty people are killed.
1998	El Niño season causes flooding in California.
1999	Rains from Hurricanes Dennis and Floyd cause flooding in North Carolina, killing fifty-two.
2004	The Indian Ocean tsunami occurs on December 26.
2005	The incomplete death toll from the Indian Ocean tsunami numbers somewhere between 200,000 and 300,000 people.

Glossary

condense—to turn into a liquid, often as a result of cooling

crest—the top of a wave

dam—a strong barrier built across a stream or river to hold back water

debris—an accumulation of rock fragments or other natural materials

diversion dam—a human-made wall that redirects or controls the flow of a river

downgrade—to lower something in power, strength, or value

earthquake—a shaking or tremor of the earth after a shifting of the Earth's crust

El Niño—waters along the equator in the Pacific Ocean that are warmer than normal

eye—the calm center part of a tropical storm or hurricane

flash flood—a flood that occurs very quickly and with extreme force

flood—a great flow of water onto normally dry land

floodplain—the level land along a river or stream that usually experiences flooding

hurricane—a storm with winds of at least 74 miles (119 km) per hour that usually develops near the western Atlantic Ocean

hydroelectricity—electricity made with the power of water

hydrometeorologist—a scientist who studies meteorology (the study of the atmosphere, weather, and weather forecasting) and hydrology (study of Earth's waters) in order to predict floods

hydropower—power made by hydroelectricity

levee—an embankment to prevent or confine flooding

precipitation—rain, sleet, hail, or snow

reservoir—an artificial lake where water is collected as a water supply

river flood—a flood caused by a river overflowing its normal limits

river stage—the height of a river measured against a fixed point

rivulet—a small stream

runoff—water that flows across the land after a rainstorm

snowmelt—runoff created by melting snow

storage dam—a human-made wall that holds back water for the purpose of saving the water for future use

storm-surge flood—a flood caused by an abnormal rise in sea level accompanying a hurricane or tropical storm

tributary—a small stream or river that flows into a larger stream or river

tropical storm—a storm near the equator with wind speeds that are more than 39 miles (63 km) per hour and less than 74 miles (119 km) per hour

tsunami—a series of large sea waves caused by an underwater earthquake or a volcanic eruption

vortex—a rotating mass of air in a column or spiral

water cycle—the process of liquid water changing to water vapor from the sun's heat, then cooling and condensing into clouds to fall again as rain

water vapor—the gas form of water

To Find Out More

Books

Allen, Jean. *Floods.* Mankato, MN: Capstone Press, 2001.

Bredeson, Carmen. *The Mighty Midwest Flood: Raging Rivers.* Berkeley Heights, NJ: Enslow Publishers, 1999.

Deedrick, Tami. *Floods.* New York: Raintree/Steck Vaughn, 2000.

Durham, Emma, and Mark Maslin. *Floods.* New York: Raintree/Steck Vaughn, 2000.

Keller, Ellen. *Floods!* New York: Simon Spotlight, 1999.

Videos and DVDs

Flood!, PBS NOVA, WGBH Video, 1996.

Johnstown Flood, Inecom Entertainment Company, 2003.

Storm Force Floods, The Learning Channel Video, 1999.

Organizations and Online Sites

American Red Cross: Flood and Flash Flood
http://www.redcross.org/services/disaster/keepsafe/readyflood.html
Run by the American Red Cross, the service organization that helps people when disaster strikes, this site provides information about what to do in flood emergencies.

Federal Emergency Management Agency (FEMA)
http://www.fema.gov/kids/floods
FEMA is responsible for helping people before and after a disaster. Its site for kids has tips for preparing a disaster survival supply kit along with photographs of various floods.

Johnstown, Pennsylvania, Information Source Online
http://www.johnstownpa.com/History/hist30.html
This site has *New York Times* newspaper articles about the Johnstown flood and photographs that show the damage left behind.

National Oceanic and Atmospheric Administration's National Weather Service

http://weather.gov/

This site has national maps outlining current warnings and forecasts for various weather events. Check out all the latest weather information for your city or town.

NOVA Online: Flood!

http://www.pbs.org/wgbh/nova/flood/

At this site, you'll find detailed information about river flooding as well as many informative links.

PBS, INFOCUS—Floods!

http://www.pbs.org/newshour/infocus/floods.html

On this page, young people from around the world tell about their personal experiences with floods. Photographs and maps are included.

The Weather Channel

http://www.weather.com/encyclopedia/flood/history.html

The Weather Channel Web site is loaded with flood information, which is part of their Storm Encyclopedia, including flood climatology (or how floods develop) and historic floods.

A Note on Sources

Research for this book began in a most traditional way—at my local library. Like many nonfiction writers, I relied on information from various reference materials, periodicals, and books. I then used this information as a jumping-off point to research specific floods.

It is hard to imagine writing such a book without the Web. For example, government Web sites have information about many natural disasters, including floods. These Web sites help locate facts and figures not yet printed in book form. I was able to obtain the latest detailed information about the Indian Ocean tsunami of December 26, 2004, from online government sites and news sources.

Videos were also helpful in preparing this book. I viewed specials on television about the immense and often dangerous power of floods. These programs are also available on video. Seeing the rising floodwaters in action, as well as the damage left behind, helped bring the topic of floods to life.

—*Lisa Trumbauer*

Index

Numbers in *italics* indicate illustrations.

Aswan High Dam, 18

Beaches, 7, 9, 24, *51*
Blizzards, 33, 44

Condensation, 13
Crests, 9

Dams, 8, 12, 19, *34–35*, 35, 36, 37, *38*, *39*, 40, 51
Debris floods, 20, *20*
Dikes, 37
Diversion dams, 37–38

Earth, *6*, 9, 12, 13, 15
Earthquakes, 10, 11
El Niño, *24*, 31, *31*, 33, *33*
Eye of hurricane, 27

Farms, 7, *14*, 15–16, *16*, 18, 29, 30, *30*
Federal Emergency Management Agency (FEMA), 37, 48–49
500-year floods, 29
Flash floods, 21–23, *21*, 51
Flash-flood warnings, 51
Flash-flood watches, 51
Floodplains, 18–19
Flood warnings, 51

Galveston, Texas, 27
Glaciers, 12
Gravity, 9
Great Flood of 1993, 23, *23*

Huang He, 50
Hurricane Dennis, 28

Hurricane Floyd, 28–29, *28*, 30
Hurricanes, 8, 25–29, *26*, *28*, 30, 44
Hydroelectricity, 38
Hydrometeorologists, 45–48
Hydropower, 38

Ice-jam floods, 19–20
India, 11
Indian Ocean tsunami, 8, 10, *10*, 11
Indonesia, 11

Johnstown Flood, 41, *41*

Kissimmee River, *48*

Lakes, 12, 51
Levees, 19, 35, 36, 37
Little Conemaugh River, 41

Malaysia, 11
Mississippi River, 23, *34–35*
Mud slides, *32*, 33

National Weather Service, 45

Neuse River, 29
Nile River, *18*, 19
Nitrogen, 13

Oxygen, 13

Pamlico River, 29
Precipitation. *See* rainfall; snow.
Puddles, 16

Rainfall, 7, 8, 12, 15–16, 17, 19, 22, 23, 32, 33, 38, 41, 43, *44*, 46, 47
Rapid Creek, 22
Reservoirs, 38, *38*, 39
River Forecast Centers, 45
River stages, 46
Rivers, 7, 12, 15–23, 17, *18*, 19, 29, *34–35*, 36, *36*, 37–38, 39, 40, 41, *42*, 46, *48*, 50, 51
Rivulets, 12, 17
Roanoke River, 29
Runoff water, 17, 23, 46

Seawalls, 51
Snow, 8, 17, 33, 38, 46
South Fork Dam, 41

Sri Lanka, *10*, 11
Storage dams, 37–38
Storm-surge floods, 27
Streams, 12

Tar River, 29
Teton Dam, 39–40, *39*
Teton River, 39
Thailand, 11
Tropical cyclones, 28
Tropical Storm Dennis, 28
Tropical storms, 26, 27, 28
Tsunamis, 8, 10, *10*, 11
Typhoon Aere, *50*
Typhoons, 28

Vortex of hurricane, 26–27

Water cycle, 13, *13*
Water jams, 19–20, 21
Water vapor, 13
Waterfalls, 12, *12*
Waves, 9, *9*, 10, 11, *24*, 33,
    50, 51
Wind, 9
World Meteorological
    Association, 30
Yellow River, 50
Yellowstone River, *42*
Yosemite National Park, *12*

About the Author

The author of nearly two hundred books for kids, Lisa Trumbauer remembers when Hurricane Floyd reached her home state of New Jersey and flooded several communities. (Luckily, her neighborhood was not affected.) The author enjoys researching and writing about any and all topics, and when not traveling or going to Orioles baseball games, she can usually be found at her computer. The author lives in New Jersey with her husband, Dave, her dog, Blue, and her cats, Cosmo and Cleo.